PREHISTORY IN BRITTANY

Menhirs and Dolmens

by Pierre-Roland GIOT

Photographs by Dominique LE DOARÉ and Daniel SORET

English translation by Jean-Paul TRUDE

ÉDITIONS D'ART
JOS LE DOARÉ
29150 - CHATEAULIN

The Champs-de-Callac menhir, at Saint-Gilles-Vieux-Marché (Côtes d'Armor).
A block of local schist 4 metres high on small predominant plateau.

Menhirs and Dolmens

THE STONE

Half way down the slope on the side of a small track twisting down the hill, stands a white coloured mass amongst the undergrowth. On approaching, one is surprised to find, not the trunk of an old tree, but an enormous standing stone, rounded and covered with moss on one side and rough and unsymmetrical on the other sides. Twice as high as a man, this block weighing about six tons, symbolising a thousand years of stability, rises proudly towards the sky. Seen from another angle, standing out against the horizon, it reminds one of a upright human silhouette turned into stone. At night it might well frighten the belated traveller.

Lost amongst the countryside, this rock is certainly not there as a result of an evil spell by some group or other protesting against the development of tourism, or a town council wanting to erect some kind of memorial. Nor was it bought from a modern-day Obélix to decorate the front lawn or satisfy the misplaced romantic dreams of a member of the local bourgeoisie. It is an authentic antique monument in its proper place, the only place where it has any sense.

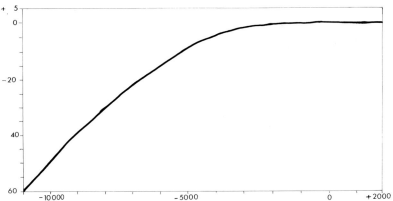

The Penloïc menhir (or Penglaouic) at Loctudy (Finistère), on the edge of the
estuary of the Pont-L'Abbé river, sticks up 4 metres above the mud flats. The
visible base is about 0. 75 metres above the actual average sea level and the
real base 0. 50 metres below this level. The graph shows the average rise in
sea level, caused by the melting ice-pack, since the last Ice Age, showing that
this menhir was erected in Neolithic times on dry land.

STANDING STONES

This upright stone is not there naturally but as a result of human intervention. It is indeed a monument, despite its rough and simple appearance. The archaeological remains found at its base allow one to situate it in the sequence of successive prehistoric civilisations. The men who erected the stone were already cultivating cereals, making fired pottery, polishing hard and resistant rocks, but still splitting flint. They were sedentary, lived in villages of wood and mud huts; they reared livestock, but still hunted, fished and gathered wild fruit. By radiocarbon dating methods on grains of charcoal, it can be established, depending on the case, that between 7, 000 and 4, 000 years have passed since these stones were erected. This corresponds to the civilisations of what archaeologists call the Neolithic period.

Wandering across the Breton moors or through the countryside, near the coast or along the inland ridges and hills, in woods and near valleys, one can seen many of these monuments, but they are also found in many other regions of Western Europe.

A closer examination shows that the base of the stone is set a few decimetres into the ground and jammed in by small stones. The monolith would slowly tip over if the stones were removed. Sometimes, fragments of rough pottery, splinters of flint, pieces of simple millstones, or a stone axe have been found in the bottom of these holes. Some of these stones have signs of burning and remains of charcoal are present, indicating that the erection ceremony was accompanied by a fire.

At the end of the XVIIIth century, over-enthusiastic archaeologists bestowed on them the name of menhir, using one of the Breton terms, although in that language the word peulvan, a more popular and at least as widely used word was better suited to the description of these veritable pillars of stone. Because of the use of these Breton words for these monuments, many people believe that they are specifically Breton, although it is certain that they are more frequent in this part of Europe. The menhirs are more often sited on slopes than on hilltops. There are some at the bottoms of valleys, and also a whole series of single menhirs are sited beside springs or along the courses of streams. These monoliths can be alone, associated with burial monuments, or with other standing stones. Sometimes they even form complex monuments, which may themselves be connected with a yet more intricate construction. They were always integrated into the surrounding countryside in which they had a role to play, being visible at least in some directions. Many have been destroyed, especially in the last two thousand years, therefore it is difficult to judge the relationship between each of them and their relationship to their geographical setting after such carnage. It should be noted that they were sometimes struck by lightning and if one extrapolates over thousands of years the partial destruction caused by lightning over the last fifty years, it is apparent that this is one reason for their disappearance as well as the iconoclastic or disrespectful madness of the generations of men that have succeeded since their construction.

Their shape varies a great deal according to the rock from which they are made. Usually they are upright oblongs. A natural block of stone, which had been isolated by erosion and which answered the purpose, was used just as it was or perhaps roughly fashioned. Quartz, quartzite or conglomerate blocks were very irregular and limited in size. The more resistant schist blocks were jagged. Granite was the most suitable and preferred rock. Amongst the chaos of granite boulders blocks could already be of the size and shape necessary. A rock however slightly protruding could be removed from the earth; on one side it shows a fresh break, on the other side an eroded surface. This explains the appearance of so many granite menhirs, which are rounded except on one side as does the presence of "giants caldrons" and other forms of natural erosion in extraordinary positions. The blocks must have been extracted in splitting the joints of the rock, by the method of traditional granymen who used to cause swelling of wedges of dry wood in slots, which had been grooved out by hammering.

In Brittany there are several menhirs which are so regular that they have obviously been shaped. They are usually very large monuments. One example is the menhir at Champ-Dolent, near Dol (Ille-et-Vilaine), which is 9.50m high, the leaning one at Saint-Samson-sur-Rance (Côtes d'Armor) 7 metres high, and in the Léon area of Finistère those of Saint Gonvarc'h at Landunvez (6m high), Kérenneur of Kerhouezel at Porspoder (6.50m), the horizontal menhir (10.50m long) and the upright menhir (9m high) at Kergadiou, Plourin-Ploudalmézeau; the latter is the most perfectly shaped specimen not only seen on its wide sides but especially on its narrow sides. Finally, the menhir at Kerloas (or Kervéatous), Plouarzel (10m high) is the tallest standing menhir.

Generally speaking, the size of the menhirs varies widely, ranging from a few decimetres up to more than 20m, the huge menhir at Locmariaquer (Morbihan) which is now broken, must have been intentionally pulled down, we shall see, like other ones, not long after having been erected. The largest menhirs still standing go up to 10 or 12m in height (root included) and must weigh several thousands of kilograms each. The menhir at Locmariaquer weighed a possible 300 tonnes, and the one on the Ile Melon at Porspoder (Finistère), 7m high, which was destroyed during the last war, weighed almost 80 tonnes.

In most instances a nearby rock was used, and transportation in this case was minimal, although still a feat of strength. Near the menhir of Men-Marz at Pontusval, Brignogan (Finistère), which is 10m. high, the rocks, from which it was removed, can be seen. There are a certain number of instances where it has been proved geologically that transportation took place over a distance as great as 3 to 4 kms (such as the monuments of Plouarzel and Dol, already mentioned). These operations were certainly carried out on rollers, using the flattest routes possible by taking the weight off each end of the stone alternately, using wooden poles to move it crabwise without having to raise the entire weight of the stone. Transport by water with the stone hung underneath a raft reduced by a third the effort required.

There are few megaliths with a flat base, simply lying in equilibrium. Most were set in the ground : the hole being dug, one tipped the block in, if necessary rolled along an embanked mound in notable raising, this embankment being destroyed after the definitive packing in. For the menhirs of small or

On the top left is the Champ-Dolent menhir at Dol-de-Bretagne (Ille-et-Vilaine) which is 9.5 metres high and of granite from about 4.5 kms away. According to legend the moon eats a piece every night and the Last Judgment will come when it completely disappears into the ground. On the top right is the Caillouan-en-Plésidy menhir (Côtes d'Armor), 7.5 metres high. Bottom left is the Créac'h-Coulm-en-Pédernec (Côtes d'Armor), 7.5 metres high. Bottom right is the menhir of the Virgin on Hoedic Island (Morbihan), which is 4 metres high.

medium weight, sheer-legs of wooden trunks could help. For the ropes, lianas such as clematite would have procured solid strands.

In the districts without natural rocks, wood may have replaced stone.

It is very rare to find figurations on the menhirs. It would appear that originally many standing stones might have been decorated, but because of being exposed to the elements, erosion has been responsible for their disappearance. Granite in particular peels of grain by grain (many eroded standing stones may have lost several inches due to erosion). Others may have been painted or served as an inside framework for a covering of woven branches and vegetable fibres.

Some examples however are known : five snakes at Le Manio at Carnac (Morbihan), axes with hafts at Saint-Denec, Porspoder (Finistère), and with crooks at Kermarquer, Moustoirac (Morbihan). On the great broken menhir at Locmariaquer there are very eroded engravings of an axe with haft or an axe-plough.

It has recently been shown that the covering slabs at Gavrinis, of the Table des Marchands and another neighbouring tumuli come from a great 14 metre stele, decorated with two bovine-type animals and axe-ploughs with hafts, which was broken into several pieces

The menhirs of Kergadiou in Plourin-Ploudalmezeau (Finistère). On the left in the background is the fallen menhir, 11 metres long in all. The fine standing stone, 9 metres high, is seen here on its wide side which is perfectly smooth.

Le Cloître Saint-Thégonnec.

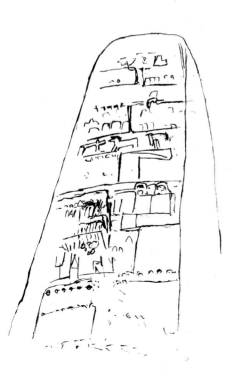

The leaning standing stone of la Tremblais in Saint-Samson-sur-Rance (Côtes d'Armor) is reputed to be a plug to Hell not properly replaced by Saint Samson and Saint Michel. The quartz veins that cross it are said to be the Devil's craw-marks. The upper and two side faces show when lit with grazing sunshine engravings that were discovered on the 22nd of August 1972 : crooks and hafted axes and a series of rectangular designs. The motifs in and between these are more difficult to interpret. "Axe-ploughs" are visible preceded by small animal figures.

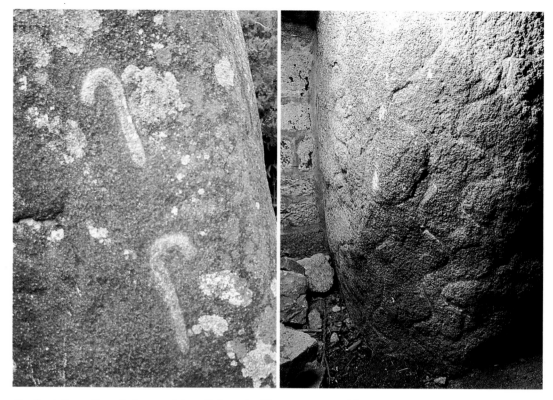

On the left are "crooks" carved in relief on the Kermarquer menhir near Moustoirac (Morbihan). To the right are "snakes" engraved on the foot of the menhir of the Manio mound at Carnac (Morbihan). These are the two techniques of decoration found on megalithic monuments.

and then dispersed. Other covering slabs of Locmariaquer, decorated or not, also appear to come from the breaking up of similar steles.

The fine leaning menhir of Saint-Samson-sur-Rance displays on its uppermost side a whole series of diagrams of rectangles with appendices, just visible by sunlight at noon, with crooks and axe-ploughs with haft between the diagrams, and even more surprising, the axe-ploughs appear to be pulled by animals; the lateral faces also have the same kinds of decoration. Erosion makes the

reading of these decorations difficult and the curves do not permit simultaneous deciphering of the whole.

Cup-marks are more common, found singly or in groups, on stones off all ages, although these are sometimes merely the effect of nature.

It is important not to confuse the megaliths with steles, whose shapes are clearly geometric, and which are common to the whole of Western Brittany. These steles date from the Iron Age and have in many cases been "Christianized".

ENCLOSURES AND MEGALITHIC ALIGNMENTS

The complex groups of standing stones fall loosely into 2 categories : alignments and enclosures, which are sometimes also connected. The stones which form these grouped monuments are not as large as the single standing stones, and for the most part have been left in their natural state. It is possible that earth embankments or ramps completed the ensemble, but these, being more vulnerable, have in most cases disappeared. It remains to be seen if there was any relationship with the erection of the stones, or if on the contrary earth embankments separating fields have not covered the remains of stone lines that were in the way, as is often the case.

True megalithic enclosures are not very frequent in Brittany, not to be confused with slabs surrounding a tumulus or funeral mound. One might ask the question concerning the curious elliptical enclosure of adjoining stones that was discovered below the neolithic tumulus of Tossen-Keler in Penvénan (Côtes d'Armor), and rebuilt in a garden on the quayside at Tréguier, as to whether it was originally open to the elements for it clearly includes some stones taken from megalithic tombs that had been dismantled. The possible destruction of its eastern end does not stop one noticing that its plan was very geometrical. Some enclosures exist in the form of a quadrilateral, but for example, the Manio quadrilateral at Carnac is almost certainly the surrounding of a tumulus like mound. The Crucuno quadrilateral at Erdeven lies exactly along the cardinal points, with its diagonals orientated towards the rising and setting sun, unless of course it was the result of over enthusiastic and over inspired restoration. Stone circles, which are numerous in the British Isles, are rarer on the continent. It is certain that they are represented in Brittany by the two ovoids or flattened tangential circles of the island of Er-Lannic at Arzon (Morbihan), the restoration of which has unfortunately changed the shape too much.

One is now partially under water because of the continual rise in the sea level since the end of the Ice Age. Associated with the circle, there are many traces of neolithic industrial and cultural activities. In fact the small number of remaining or supposed enclosures is quite surprising, even taking into account those that were constructed entirely of wood that have disappeared without any known trace. It must be assumed that succeeding cultures destroyed them.

The Crucuno quadrilateral.
A part of the semi-circle of adjoining stones of the system of alignments to the
South of Saint-Pierre-Quiberon (Morbihan).

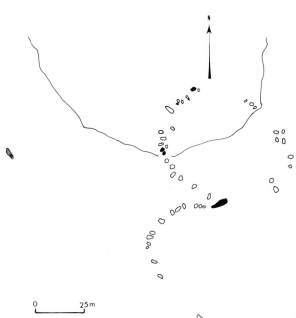

0   25m

The "circle" of standing stones visible from the air on the small island of Er-Lannic in the Morbihan Gulf. Plan of the two tangent circles before restoration of the visible part. The exact plan of the original monument remains uncertain. The lowest stone is situated about one metre below today's lowest low tide level.

13

The Menec alignments at Carnac seen from the western end. In the foreground can be seen the last stones of the chord of the semi-circle or oval occupied by the village. At the top of the photo the change in orientation is noticeable, situated in the middle of the field of alignments.

14

Two general categories of megalithic lines are discernible. Firstly large fields formed by several parallel rows of standing stones or blocks, arranged in diminishing size although it seems that in a complete monument the size increased again towards the other end. But truly complete monuments no longer exist. In the examples still intact the rows move off at right angles to an oval of menhirs placed edge to edge. The most famous monuments are at Carnac. At Le Menec, there are still 1,169 stones in existence, 70 of which are arranged in an oval amongst the houses and gardens of the village, and 1,099 in lines, with an average width between the lines of 100m. and the lines are 1,167m long finishing with the dilapidated remains of a second oval enclosure, of which 25 stones still remain. In the middle of the field formed by the lines, the orientation changes distinctly. At Kermario, 982 stones remain (1, 029 have sometimes been counted), grouped in ten main lines over an average width of 100 metres and a length of 1, 120 metres, with many complexities of different orientations and partial lines as well as a transversal line; but there are no remains of the oval enclosure at the west end nor any indications at the other end. At Kerlescan 594 menhirs remain, 30 of which are in an oval (the holes for several others have been found), and 555 in 13 lines, 880m long and 139m apart from the main section extended at a different angle by several rows. These 3 principal fields follow on from each other with gaps of about 250 and 400m, while at the same time changing direction.

Answering a question that is often asked, stones that have been put upright again in recent times have been marked with a small square hole in the base filled with pink cement.

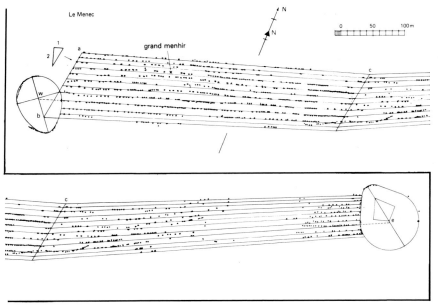

PLAN OF THE MENEC ALIGNMENTS
according to A. Thom.

The small alignment of Saint-Denec near Porspoder (Finistère) consists of two menhirs still standing and two lying on the ground. On the stone in the foreground two rough relief carvings of hafted axes are visible.

What remains of the Demoiselles alignments of Langon (Ille-et-Vilaine), the dancers turned into stone.

*One of the lines of the alignments called "The Stone Wedding" at Brasparts
(Finistère), once again, dancers turned into stone.*
*The Lagatjar alignments at Camaret (Finistère) consisting of three crossing
lines of different orientations.*

Other important alignments also exist in Morbihan in the Carnac area. At Kerzehro, Erdeven, there are 1,129 stones in 10 lines in the main section. At Sainte-Barbe, Plouharnel and Le Moulin de Saint-Pierre-Quiberon there are some ovalshaped remains as well as some rows of standing stones. Only the ovoid is still in existence at Kergonan on the Ile-aux-Moines.

But the Carnac area is not the only place where monuments like these, with several rows of stones are found. They also exist in other areas of Brittany : Pleslin (Côtes-d'Armor), Langon (Ille-et-Vilaine), Penmarc'h (Finistère) : the latter ensemble, which consisted of almost 500 stones, is almost completetly in ruins. There are groups of stones arranged in 2 parallel rows in the British Isles but these do not seem to have developed on the continent.

The simple alignments, consisting either of one single line or of several lines at different angles, which therefore intersect each other, are studded profusely all over the Armorican peninsula. Most of them consist of a few stones only for example those in the Montagnes Noires, which have suffered much damage (Tri Men, the three stones, at Saint-Goazec are the most visible). Among the most striking examples are the ones at Grée-de-Cojoux at Saint-Just (Ille-et-Vilaine) and Lagatjar at Camaret (Finistère), or again the ones at Saint-Michel of Brasparts (Finistère). Recent excavations at Saint-Just have shown, in the southern line, the association of wooden poles with the standing stones, in the midst of complex successive structures. A little further a line of standing stones has been observed set in a long bed of small stones, a kind of roadway or a very low tumulus, superimposed on pathed fire-places, dated by radiocarbon methods at between 5, 000 and 4, 000 years B.C., when some menhirs may have been erected. A fire-place beneath the Kersolan alignments at Languidic (Morbihan) has been dated a few centuries more recent.

All over Western Europe, wherever there are standing stones, there are alignments. But these were not restricted to the stones who survive nowadays.

A line of the Grand-Resto and Kersolan alignments at Languidic (Morbihan), a large ensemble that has suffered much damage.

Two stones of the transversal line to the north of Kerzerho near Erdeven (Morbihan).

One of the two lines of the Moulin-de-Cojoux alignments at Saint-Just (Ille-et-Vilaine) after excavations and restoration. The stones were originally set in a base of small stones above very ancient fire-places.

The pair of the great (7,5 metres high) and the small menhir of Pergat near Louargat (Côtes d'Armor). On the ground are natural blocks or fallen standing stones.

Two stones are enough to mark out a bearing. If there are more, they are almost superfluous, complicate matters and diminish the accuracy, although one can never be sure of the exact vertical position intended for a massive and bulky stone. The problem of the bearings of the megalithic monuments, which has been studied for more than a century, has been confounded by fanciful theories, and serious work, which is based on less disputable, even carefully sifted facts, has shared the general opprobrium. To begin with they were interpreted as being approximate solar, solstitial or equinoctial calendars, and later, somewhat haphazardly as stellar or lunar calendars, and of course here and there some did correspond to these theories. It is quite possible that something of that sort did exist, but much less precise than we might imagine. According to certain fashionable hypotheses, these monuments would represent diverse elements of large observatories for predicting eclipses. In spite of tentatives of sophisticated demonstrations, nothing has up to now been validly proved. The same uncertainty exists about the use of units, of geometrical figures or of quasi geodetical arrangements. It is too easy to believe appearances of approximative coincidences which prove nothing.

All these data do not in the end throw much light on the reason for the standing stones, which remain shrouded in deep mystery. It is perhaps just as well, because who knows, as we learn from unusual discoveries of comparative ethnological studies throughout the world, we might well learn horrible things (undoubtedly different from things suggested a few centuries ago) that would make our stones a lot less attractive. This is probably why the study of these stones has been comparatively neglected, quite wrongly. Attempts have sometimes been made to interpret them by a comparative study of the legends which have survived to our day, but with no very significant results. That would imply too much continuity between the populations which succeeded each other. We can simply conclude that they are symbolic or religious monuments. This vague title, which is very easy to suggest, is a way of cloaking our ignorance.

The standing stones related to the worship of the gods, and especially to the chief symbol of the gods among primitive and half-civilized peoples : the Sun, which dies and is reborn each day. Indeed, among the deities of the builders of the megaliths, the sun must have played a prominent role, as various signs lead us to believe. But it must not be forgotten either that the Moon plays an important part in primitive calendars, which are usually based on both the sun and the moon. The ability to predict eclipses is obviously very prestigious for the priesthood whose divining powers were much esteemed and where clairvoyance and mediation were the requisite qualities in all societies. Finally, the often very suggestive shape of many standing stones, as of that of similar standing stones in Africa or Asia, has given rise to the belief, probably well founded, that they symbolized fertility, the representation of which is easily linked with the sun, the lifegiver of all things.

But for the modern symbolic archeologists, these stones represent people, and not gods. They might as well symbolise the power of chiefs or of ancestors.

THE MEGALITHIC TOMBS

The cult of the dead was the other important ritual element among the prehistoric peoples, even if this veneration is intended as a means of protection against any eventual malediction from the deceased. This is why the other megalithic monuments which were used as tombs, were dedicated to this cult. Funeral rites, often lavish, testify to a belief, if not in complete immortality, at least in metempsychosis or reincarnation and also that the dead had powers, be they good or evil. The more or less stylized figures on the walls of certain tombs, of another goddess of fertility, the mothergoddess or great goddess, as well as the custom of leaving personal effects in the tomb for use on the great journey in the future life, implies the idea of rebirth.

Standing stones had a masculine and celestial connotation, whereas megalithic graves were associate more with the earth-mother, and like grottos and everything that was underground, had a feminine signification.

Contrary to contemporary burial customs, in Eastern Europe, Central Europe and Mediterranean Europe, where there was a tradition of individual graves, more often than not with the body in a sitting or crouched position (recalling that of the foetus) rather than a lying position, isolated or grouped together in a necropolis, the first megalithic tombs, where of course the bones have survived, show that they were collective tombs and served as "family vaults" for a community over several generations even if only selected individuals had the right to be there.

That being so, it does however appear that things are much more complicated than that. The idea of a simple grave is more or less replaced by the notion of a "house of the dead" or "house of ancestors" or a kind of temple dedicated to the life-sustaining earth and acting as a central gathering point for a whole community.

DIFFERENT TYPES OF MEGALITHIC TOMBS

Contrary to an individual grave where the deceased occupies a small hole which is then filled in or a small coffer or stone box where the body is in a crouched position, therefore taking up no more space than a modern coffin, collective burial chambers are much bigger in size. Two basic types of neolithic burial chambers are distinguishable.

1° Burial caves, which could simply be a natural cave adapted for this use. Indeed, it was often thought that all this burial architecture is an imitation of natural caves. Where natural caves did not exist, it was possible, when the rock was soft enough, to dig artificial caves (in chalk for example, in the Champagne region). In Brittany there are none of either kind. It was thought that because the substrata rocks were too hard, earth mounds were built covering a construction which imitated a natural cave. However, this satisfactory explanation is marred by some chronological and geological difficulties, when Europe as a whole is considered. One might even wonder whether it could be reversed because in fact tombs carved in rock appear later and are imitations of megalithic tombs that existed much earlier.

2° Burial chambers built on the ground, generally covered with earth (mound or tumulus) or stones (cairn) to make them weather-proof, which in some ways resemble a natural cave. However their detailed construction using slabs or blocks of stone show similarities of plan and building methods with those used by the same builders to construct their own houses using wood, wattle and daub, examples of which are well known in some regions. Houses for the living were built to last a limited time and were reasonably comfortable, whereas houses for the dead were built to last forever.

Usually, if rock exists on the site or nearby, the artificial crypts are formed of huge flat stones, whence the justified name of megalithic chambered tombs. But a construction partially or completely made up of smaller stones may also be used. Thus the habit has arisen of calling "megaliths" monuments which do not justify this title, although they are connected with the same type of civilization and the total mass of material used are fundamently similar.

Both Man's powers of adaptation and at the same time his vis inertiae must be taken into account. In areas where it would have been easy to dig artificial caves, this was not done. In other areas wood may have been used, even if only for covering beams. There are no traces left of this. Also, some monuments which now appear to be incomplete or in ruins were perhaps partly constructed of wood. In any event, an enormous amount of wood was needed for the construction, rollers, scaffolding and levers etc, required during the placing of the slabs. The regions where megaliths are not found are often regions where lasting methods of construction were almost impossible. It has been observed in Brittany at least that the density of standing stones and megalithic tombs relates directly to the nature of the terrain and the proximity of raw materials. In the inland areas of schistous subsoil rock, for example, there are small quartz standing stones. Where there are remains of a gallery grave, because a harder and more resistant type of schist was used, details reminiscent of the art of carpentry can often be observed, schist being workable to a certain extent.

Some indisputable instances of transportation can be geologically proved. The most famous and the most important example is probably one of our finest monuments, la Roche-aux-Fées at Essé (Ille-et-Vilaine). The subsoil is precambrian schist, very soft and weathered. This edifice was built of purple cambrian schist, the nearest outcrop of which is 4.2 kms away, and these stones were probably obtained even further away. About 40 slabs were used. The capstones are particularly massive; half a dozen of them must weigh about 40-50 tonnes each. Yet however impressive transportation on such a scale might seem, it only touches the immediate edges of a region of rocks which are just as suitable.

Whether over short or long distances, the process must have been the same : inclined planes, levers and rollers, wedges, ropes.

Advancing crab-like, by pulling alternatively on each end of a large block, economised the effort of lifting; do we not use the same method to move a heavy piece of furniture when we are short of helping

The Roche-aux-Fées near Essé (Ille-et-Vilaine) consists of a large partitioned chamber preceded by a anti-chamber with a monumental porch-like entrance. The monument is orientated roughly towards the rising sun at the winter solstice.

0 _____ 5 m

hands. To roll the capstones into position, the tumulus, or at least a mound, was piled up until it was level with the top of the vertical supports. There has been a great deal of discussion as to whether all these monuments were originally covered with a tumulus, as most of them are now completely exposed. This exposure is quite possibly due to natural erosion as well as damage by man, particularly in the name of culture, in the case of earth tumuli as well as for the cairns, which have been used as a source of stones for paving roads or construction of dry-stone walls. In a few exceptional cases, the ramps which were essential for the erection may have been removed after use.

If the builders of megalithic tombs built them to last forever, the least that can be said is that after a certain number of generations their descendants might not have had the same scrupulous respect for such heritage. They might well have destroyed a monument (like the great steles of Locmariaquer, for example) and reused the materials to build other monuments, once again built to last forever. More often though, the monuments were re-worked, transformed, modified or extended and sometimes they were already in need of repair. The final appearance of the monument might thus become very different from the original plan, as is the case of so many of our medieval monuments. Yet in the case of many big and complex monuments, such as the great cairn of Barnenez in Plouézoc'h, it is apparent that great care has been taken to continue the original architectural structure and maintain the overall aesthetic appearance. We are talking hear, of architectural monuments and not heaps of stones. One of the architectural constraint might be the orientation, comparatively delicate in the case of lines of standing stones. The entrances of megalithic tombs are not very precisely orientated. In Normandy there are cairns with tombs in a star disposition. But it is fairly common, probably because of the climate, to find them facing East or South that is towards one third of the compass-card. Another reason for a particular orientation might be that the tomb entrance faces a particular part of the countryside that is it especially supposed to command and protect.

A whole series of architectural variations are noticeable among the megalithic tombs, which can be classified more or less artificially in typological families to which have been given rather badly chosen names and which we would now like to be rid of, if only we could break the habit of using them.

Generally speaking, similar monuments exist all over the world. They can date from all the ages in the last few 1,000 years and are therefore not necessarily of the same age and even less related in any way.

In Europe alone they form a fairly homogeneous series, in which it would be illusory to look for a relationship or an order of distribution although on a local or regional level it might be possible to do so. There have been homeric discussions as to whether different groups of European megaliths had independent origins, or on the contrary, a common origin, and if so, where. The classic view was that the tradition must have had its origin somewhere in the eastern Mediterranean, and subsequently reached the Western Mediterranean and finally Western Europe. The chronological data that we now have shows us that this view can no longer be considered : In any case, the whole megalithic civilization of Wester Europe was already in the process of development more than 6,000 years ago and must have started almost 7, 000 years ago. It is a Western invention, one might even say an Atlantic one, which owes nothing to the East.

The antiquaries of the XVIIIth century invented the term of dolmen as a name for these monuments (from the Breton taol-ven, meaning stone table), because what impressed them most was the main and sometimes enormous covering slab of many of the monuments. Whilst remembering that there are always several cap-stones and even the remplacement of the main table by a small dry-stone structure, the best use we can make of this traditional term it to use it to describe any kind of megalithic tomb. If they had wished to chose an authentic Breton term, that of lia, liac'h, lia-ven would have been preferable, although its etymology (usually translated by the Welsh Ilech) leaves much to be desired.

Within the framework of traditional typological distinctions, the first group of monuments, and on the whole the most ancient, are generally called passage-graves (dolmens à couloir), consisting essentially of a circular, polygonal or four-sided chamber, reached by a passage (also called gallery or corridor). This passage can be short, similar in length to the chamber, or it can extend considerably. When monuments of this kind are single examples, they are generally covered by compact four-sided or circular cairns or tumuli, some of which are thick and very high. There are also groups of several chambers under cairns whose forms vary according to whether the layout of the chambers is side by side or in a fan or star formation. They are spread along the south and west coast of the Iberian peninsula, side by side with artificial caves of the same type. They are found again in the Poitou region; and in large numbers along the southern coast of the Armorican peninsula. So they are found all along the coast from the Gironde to Normandy, and in several regions of the West and North of the British Isles, Ireland and Northern Europe as well as in the Netherlands and Scandinavia.

P.–R. GIOT

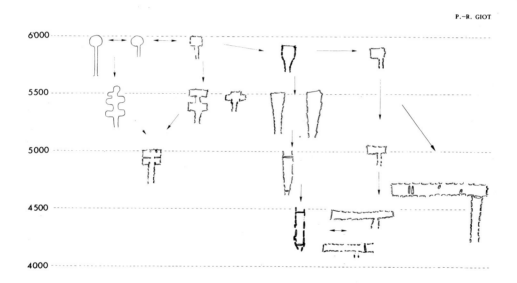

Typological and chronological relation (in years before the present) between the main types of megalithic tombs in Brittany, in an attempt to show the overall regional development. At the top left are passage-graves (long or short passages), with circular chambers of dry-stone, from which might have derived the types with lateral alcoves. Square or polygonal chambers made of slabs might have led to "transepted" types and later, partitioned chambers. When the differentiation begins between chamber and passage, this leads to the V-shaped, and then to gallery-graves. When the passage is off centre, by a lateral extension of the chamber, this leads to right-angled forms, or gallery-graves with lateral entrances.

But later forms of passage-graves found widely in the Pyrenees, in Catalonia, in the Languedoc, in Provence and in the Causses region are in fact graves of a second type.

A second group of monuments are predominantly elongated. The monuments of this category are included in or under long barrows, which barely cover the graves inside them. These graves consist of a long chamber or cist, often divided into several smaller chambers. The most specialized type of these is generally called a gallery grave or allée couverte, a rather unfortunate name, since a certain number of these tombs apparently had no roof. In Brittany hardly anything except the classic gallery-graves exists. These are found outside of Brittany, in the western part of Central France, in the Paris Basin, in Belgium and some parts of the Rhinelands such as the Hesse region and South

A part of the decorations on the reused stele found in the cairn of Mané-er-Hroek at Locmariaquer (Morbihan). Hafted axes, "U" signs and shield-shaped design.

The dolmen with lateral chambers at Mané-Groh in Erdeven (Morbihan).

The chamber of Kercadoret at Locmariaquer (Morbihan).
The earth tumulus of the angled passage-grave of Kerners in Bono (Morbihan).

Westphalia, and also in Southern Sweden. Similar types of tombs exist in the Franche-Comté region and surrounding areas, with particular forms reminiscent of those of the houses of the same period.

Of course, there are numerous types of megalithic tombs, which it is difficult to fit into either of the above categories, which are in truth fairly controversial. There are transitional, intermediary or hybrid forms, which are very interesting. Apart from modifications of form or use of certain monuments over a very long period of time, it should be remembered that over some 2 500 years after the first monuments, megalithic architecture was far from rigid, and that even geographically, there are numerous variations.

For instance, small accessory burial chambers may be grafted on to monuments of either type. Side by side with collective megalithic tombs in this region there are both collective and individual tombs of different affinities, among other groups of cists, and especially the low long barrows found inland (Saint-Just (Ille-et-Vilaine); Le Quillio (Côtes-d'Armor)), or on the coast (Carnac (Morbihan), Guérande (Loire-Atlantique)), from a neolithic tradition found also in Northern and Eastern Europe. But megalithic architectural techniques have influenced them, in Armorica, in certain aspects, such as the demarcation of the barrow by a enclosure, formed by stone slabs which are joined together, upright or leaning outwards, replacing a system of wooden stakes used in other areas.

Finally, at the same time as the construction of the collective megalithic tombs was coming to an end, and also probably after it had finished in Western Brittany, many barrows with individual chambers of the Early and Middle Bronze Ages were being erected.

The influence of megalithic architectural techniques shows in the building of vaults below the surface and no longer above it, or in small cist-like tombs which were not so deep. In these one finds all the aspects of megalithic constructions (slabs, sometimes very heavy and coming from far away; and sometimes of dry-stone) but they should not be confused with the veritable megalithic tombs.

The Liscuis gallery-grave

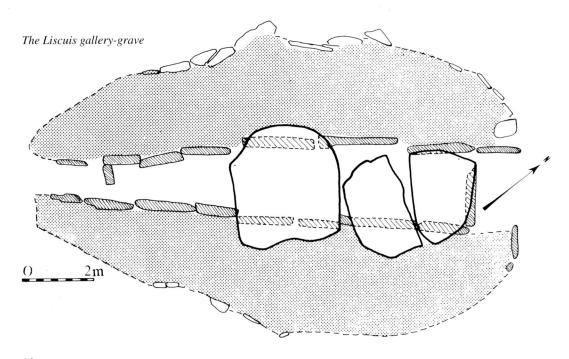

0   2m

Buttressed gallery-grave of Castel-Ruffel in Saint-Goazec (Finistère).
No 1 gallery-grave of Liscuis in Laniscat (Côtes d'Armor) seen from the apse
of its mound. A V-shaped monument reminiscent of the structure of passage-
graves.

PASSAGE-GRAVES IN BRITTANY

Let us consider the first group, the passage-graves or dolmens à couloir, their variations and derivatives. They are well represented in the Charentes region, the Poitou, including the Vendée. There are also a certain number along the Loire-Atlantique coast. To the south of the Loire, in the Retz region, there is a remarkable collection of monuments around Pornic, where one can admire the triple trapezoidal and concentric stone facings of the Mousseaux cairn, covering two monuments with "transepted" chambers. There are also remains of other monuments of this type at Clion. To the north of the Loire, on the edge of the Brière region, at Herbignac, there is another "transepted" type monument, but in general, the Brière region was surrounded by more conventional monuments such as the fine passage-grave at Kerbourg in Saint-Lyphard. At Dissignac near Saint-Nazaire, a complex cairn covers two early passage-graves set side by side. Two small concentric stone walls originally surrounded the cairn, but later, when the passages were extended, two new walls were built to limit the extended and now very spectacular cairn.

On the Rhuys peninsula, beyond the estuary of the Vilaine, as well as on the islands and shores of the Morbihan Gulf, there are many megalithic tombs. The immense dome-shaped tumulus of Tumiac near Arzon is part of this ensemble and has only been partly explored. Its successive layers of various kinds of earth cover a large closed vault in a cairn, forming the hub, and the surrounding satellite graves. At 15 metres high, its is the biggest neolithic monument in the region and contained a rich collection of grave-goods. It represents a small series of exceptional monuments, situated on both sides of the entrance to the Morbihan Gulf which were contemporary to classical passage-graves. They are evidence of a privileged political and social situation, or at least of a certain "wealth", in view of the prestige of the objects and the symbols of power, not to mention the ostentation of the size of the construction. Other monuments of the same series, but long and lower, were situated on headlands along the shores of the gulf. Facing the open sea, the complex monument of Petit-Mont, also near Arzon, suffered damage during the war. It was made up of several adjoining cairns surrounded by a series of concentric walls encompassing the whole complex. Of the two passage-graves that existed, the westerly one had uprights decorated with numerous engravings, and also a door with carved parts.

The fantastic engravings of the fine burial chamber under a cairn of the Isle of Gavrinis in Larmor-Baden make it one of the wonders of the world, or at least of the megalithic world. The cairn has recently been restored and shows that the cap-stone of the chamber comes from Locmariaquer. Also, having cleared the facing stones in front of the entrance, it appears that in the late neolithic, the entrance was blocked by a mass of stone which covered the esplanade where ceremonies used to be held, using light outdoor wooden structures. Many quartz chipping tools, used to engrave the stone slabs, were found there. On the nearby Ile Longue is another cairn, which is unfortunately not open to the public. It covers the remains of a long passage-grave, whose chamber, more-or-less intact, is circular with corbelled dry-stone walls and roof, showing that when it was impossible to obtain a large capstone for the roof, another construction technique could be used. Some of the uprights of the passage are decorated with interesting engravings.

Passage-graves are so numerous in this coastal region of the Morbihan, that it is not surprising that their builders settled in the Vannes hinterland. Some monuments are dotted along the granite ridge that is now known as the Landes de Lanvaux (Lanvaux moors). A small group of other passage tombs, far from the coast, is isolated at Saint-Just (Ille-et-Vilaine), two monuments with a circular chamber, small vertical slabs facing dry-stone walling, and also under the Château-Bú barrow, a passage-grave with two lateral

The B dolmen of the Mousseaux cairn at Pornic, with to the left its half-transept seen from inside (the A dolmen is completely "transepted").

The monumental facade of the Dissignac cairn near Saint-Nazaire (Loire-Atlantique) with the entrances to two side by side passage-graves. The extended parts of the passages do not have covering stones.

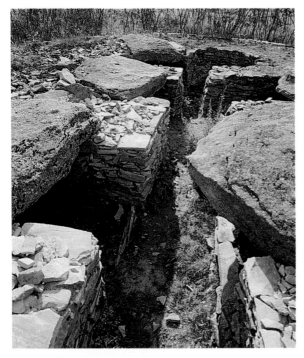

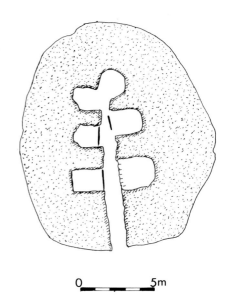

0 _____ 5m

The second cairn at Larcuste at Colpo (Morbihan) contains a passage-grave of dry-stone with a series of small chambers on each side.

expansions. Some monuments were in contact with the sea along the rivers Vilaine and Oust. For the others it was the proximity of the Morbihan Gulf that was important. The two side-by-side cairns of Larcuste at Colpo are particularly interesting because they have been excavated recently. Cairn I contains two conventional passage-graves and is surrounded by a double stone facing, whereas cairn II contains a central passage with a series of small lateral chambers.

The densest concentration of passage-graves in Morbihan is between the mouth of the gulf of Morbihan and the river Etel. This "necropolis" which is centred around Carnac and Quiberon, may have numbered several hundreds of tombs of varyings types, a good hundred of which have been preserved.

The floor of the burial chambers and of their passages is often paved. Within the general design, important variations are possible; side or lateral chamber along the passage and even small alcoves on the chamber. The extreme example of variation is that of the monuments inaccurately called angled gallery-graves and

which should be named graves with passages at right angles. These are dissymetric burial chambers where the chamber was built at right angles to the passage (Le Rocher au Bono; Les Pierres-Plates at Locmariaquer; Luffang at Crach; Mane-er Ioh at Locoal-Mendon; Gâvres).

Sometimes several burial chambers are grouped in the same cairn or the same tumulus, like the three burial chambers of Mane-Kerioned at Carnac, or the three chambers of Rondossec at Plouharnel. More often two, three or more monuments are grouped very close to each other (Kerran at Locmariaquer, Parc-Guren at Crach; Mané-Braz at Erdeven; Kerbrevost at Belz, etc.). Generally the passage-graves in this area are clearly sited, deliberately, on the top of a little hill or some rising ground, forming a vast cemetery of unrelated burials.

In this area of Morbihan particularly, the uprights of the burial chambers may be decorated by engravings on their inner sides, normally the best surfaced sides of each stone; sometimes also the underside of the

The chamber of the angled dolmen of Goërem at Gâvres (Morbihan) is partitioned. Vertical slabs alternate with dry-stone masonry.

The chamber of the Mané-Rutual dolmen at Locmariaquer (Morbihan), looking towards the ante-chamber, which is an intermediary structure before the passage itself.

Hafted axe-plough engraved on the fragment of stele used as a covering slab at the Table-des-Marchand at Locmariaquer (Morbihan).

The passage of the Kercado dolmen at Carnac, seen from the chamber. Engravings on the lateral support on the right.

cap-stones. Carvings of polished stone axes, with or without hafts, are engraved on them, also many indecipherable arabesques, of which the most simple is a "U" sign. But a large number of these figures seem to be very stylized outlines or portions of human bodies. Whether the head is reduced to a sort of pot, whose ears are the handles, with crewcut hair, or whether the whole individual only appears by the feet, it is likely that these are forms of the most frequently found goddess-protectress of the megalithic tombs, of indeterminate sex at this stage. The supporting stone often has a contour which is scroll-like or in some rare cases vaguely anthropomorphous. Along with many other dolmens, the one of Kercado at Carnac, which still has its earth mound, has fine ornamentations of this kind, as does one of the three passage-graves of Mané-Kerioned.

The dolmens of Locmariaquer deserve a special mention. Great standing stones or steles were originally erected there, bearing the same kinds of decorations on their best surfaced side.

The stones were then pulled down and cut up by another generation (the great broken standing stone was an example of this as we have seen before), and the pieces reused as capstones of some prestigious passage-graves. Thus, a fragment of a decorated stele used as a covering stone for the Table-des-Marchand (where the under-side is decorated with an axe-plough, a crook and the four feet of a animal) corresponds exactly with a fragment used to cover the chamber at Gavrinis (where the invisible outside face has the rest of the horned animal and another axe-plough). The end slab of the same Table-des-Marchand is well known for its shield-like design and its relief engravings of "crooks". The Mané-Rutual dolmen, with a chamber and anti-chamber, is covered with a piece of a stele decorated with an enormous shield-like design which would be invisible if it were not for the way it is presented today.

The angled monument of the Pierres-Plates has perhaps the finest collection of engraved stone slabs of a different style.

Engraving on the right lateral stone of the Pierres Plates dolmen at Locmariaquer.

The end of the passage of the prodigious decorated dolmen of Gavrinis, near Larmor-Baden (Morbihan).

The passage of the angled dolmen of Goërem at Gâvres (Morbihan). On the ground is the movable slab that acted as a door to the chamber.

At Locmariaquer there are enormous mounds covering closed vaults, containing fine grave-goods, which were undoubtedly the tombs of important people. The cairn at Mané-er-Hroëk is circular. Its covering stones are also fragments of a broken stele. Another small piece with exceptional decorations, found in the outside layers of the chamber and used as simple stone filling, is now exhibited in the vault near the artificial entrance that now leads into it. These enormous earth mounds can be elongated, encompassing a passage-grave at the extremity. These are associations between the closed vault and the chamber communicating with the land of the living. This is the case at Mané-Lud at Locmariaquer and also at Carnac in the monuments of Moustoir and Saint-Michel. In the latter, the central vault is surrounded by smaller satellite tombs.

The remaining monuments near the western edge of the Morbihan (including the Isle of Groix) are relatively simple constructions, but more complicated ones existed before being destroyed. Near Port-Louis, in the village of Gâvres, there is a superb right-angled dolmen, still under its original mound. At the junction of the passage and the chamber (which is incompletely subdivided into four compartments) a large slab served as a "door". The right-angled dolmen of the Rocher at Le Bono, on the left bank of the Auray River, also still has its original mound.

Passage-graves in South Finistère have suffered much damage since the last century. They existed in large numbers in the Bigouden region (around Pont-L'Abbé and Penmarc'h), another megalithic metropolis, as dense as that of the area around Carnac. Between the rivers Ellé and Odet, surviving dolmens are few and far between. However, the linked monuments of Kerleven, la Forêt-Fouesnant, must be mentionned, of a type with compartimented chamber.

The great Saint-Michel tumulus at Carnac (Morbihan), seen from the North. A chapel now stands on it.
One of the individual tombs.

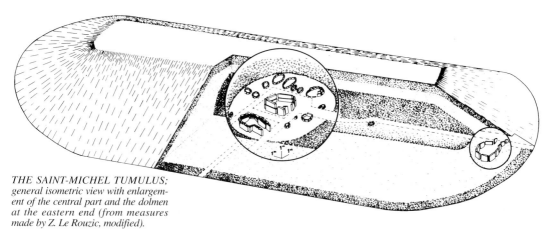

THE SAINT-MICHEL TUMULUS; general isometric view with enlargement of the central part and the dolmen at the eastern end (from measures made by Z. Le Rouzic, modified).

Many groups of monuments with partitioned chambers existed as far as the area around La Pointe du Raz, but most of them have been badly damaged. Such is the case for the one at La Pointe du Souc'h near Plouhinec. The best surviving example is at Quélarn near Plobannalec, with the incomplete remains of a group of six partitioned dolmens. On the top of La Pointe de la Torche there is a simplified partitioned dolmen, later modified by lengthening the passage.

Also, near Penmarc'h in the Bigouden region, the T-shaped dolmen at Poulguen still has a part of its earth mound and has engravings reminiscent of the scrolls of right-angled monuments of the Morbihan. The T-shaped dolmen at Kerugou no longer has any earth covering.

The dolmen of Run-Aour from Plomeur (re-erected next to the Prehistory Museum of Finistère) appears to have had two right-angled passages with a chamber of dry-stone at the junction of the passages. It was a kind of hybrid.

In the Cap-Sizun, no surviving significant burial chambers are visible, and those of the Crozon peninsula (for example Rostudel near the Cap de la Chèvre) and on the slopes of Menez-Hom are very simple, having lost their passages. In inland central Finistère, a few rare monuments are proof of localized penetration, such as the cairn at Saint-Thois with its two dolmens, one of which has a double chamber. The fine V-shaped dolmen of Ty-ar-Boudiquet near Brennilis, which has no separation between the passage and the chamber, is a forerunner of what was to become gallery-graves.

Passage-graves were more numerous along the Channel and Iroise coasts of Brittany than it was thought until recently.

Dolmens with partitioned chambers of the Saint-Laurent cairn at la Forêt-Fouesnant (Finistère).

The dolmen with partitioned chamber at la Torche near Plomeur (Finistère) seen from the West. This is quite an early monument in the series.

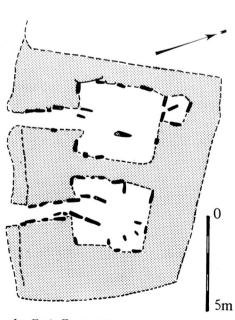

La Forêt-Fouesnant.

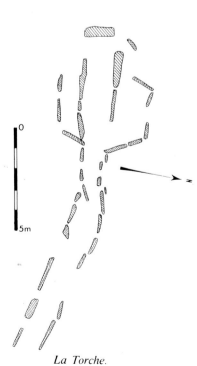

La Torche.

In fact a few have been found scattered near the landing places of intrepid seafarers, ususally on tiny islands or on peninsulas. But at the time, the sea-level being lower, some were already on the mainland. However this was not the case in the islands of the Molene archipelago, where there were many small dolmens. Forms with corbelled roofs were the most common. Often only a few vertical slabs remain, probably playing a decorative role, being as they were set in front of dry-stone walls, and even then, such ultimate remains are only visible in impossible places. Much has been lost due to activities such as the intensive vegetable growing of Upper-Léon region and the seaweed gathering of the Lower-Léon region.

When the cairn on the Ile Carn, near Ploudalmézeau, was built, it overlooked a fertile hinterland which is now bare and drowned countryside. In its original form it had a trapezoidal shape and contained three side-by-side dolmens with short passages. The chambers (the central one is intact and the others restored after recent excavations) have corbelled roofs using small thin granite slabs. After their period of use, masses of material were used to block the front and the back of the original cairn and the whole was encircled by a circular facing wall. To improve the presentation of the monument, the front blocking mass has been reduced in height to expose the passage entrances. The small island of Guennoc, in front of Landéda, also used to overlook fertile land which is now below water due to the rising sea-level. On its ridge there were three main cairns. Two of them had three dolmens with short passages. The third, with seven dolmens, was more important. With a distinct trapezoidal

The facade of the primary cairn of the great cairn of the Ile Carn in Ploudalmézeau (Finistère). The entrance to one of the passage-graves is visible.

Looking up at the corbelled roof of the central domen of the Ile Carn.

The inside of the northern chamber with its entrance.

shape, it has an extension against the wide base which contains two head to foot tombs, one of which is orientated in the opposite direction to all the others. On the small island of Roc'h-Avel, not far away, at the actual high tide limit, there are remains of a dry-stone dolmen which has suffered damage from the sea. This shows that the choice of a position on a high point of the surrounding countryside can only be relative.

Once cleared of the rubble due to the collapse of their superstructures, these trapezoidal shaped cairns reveal monumental facades. In front of these façades a terrace, parvis or esplanade was used for ceremonial purposes. A perfect example of this, and in fact for all aspects of megalithic architecture, is the extraordinary cairn of Barnenez on the highest point of the Kernéléhen peninsula at

Plouezoc'h. It overlooks the lower lands of the Morlaix Bay, which were not under water at the time of its construction. 75m long, 20-25m wide, 6-8m high, it consists of series of 11 dolmens with long passages side by side, each monument being slightly different from the one next to it. There are 9 dry-stone chambers with a vaulted false dome, some resting on uprights and others not; the passages have walls of flat stone slabs or drystone, but always with a roof of capstones. Inserted between the others there is also a more classic burial chamber entirely built of flat stones, and another which has between the chamber and the passage, entirely in slabs, an antechamber with a vaulted roof resting on uprights. Three of these monuments have engraved stones but in one case it is a reused stone. A great deal of pottery was discovered in a small area of the front parvis.

The Barnenez cairn at Plouézoc' h (Finistère) seen from the South-west.

Section of chamber D with a view of the passage.   *Section of chamber C.*

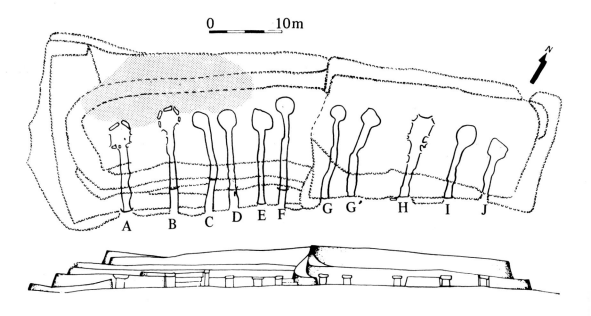

THE BUILDERS

To build one cubic metre of dry-stone masonry about 1,500 kg of rock are required, and taking into account all the work involved (extraction, shaping or splitting, putting in place, transport on the site), this could amount to 4 days work for one labourer.

The transport time from the original rock source must be added : at Barnenez the dolerite stone probably came from between 250 and 500 metres away, whereas the granite was 2 km away, or even a little more.

The hub of the primary cairn at Barnenez represents a volume of about 2,000 cubic metres of stone. Taking into account the spaces, this represents about 3,000 tons of local dolerite and about 1,000 tons of granite.

If we suppose that it was built in a single campaign, which is in fact doubtful, and we do not consider any "added-values" concerning the capstones, we can estimate the building time at between 15,000 and 20,000 days, that is between 150,000 and 200,000 man-hours at 10 hours per day. 200 men, or 300 if we allow for unexpected problems, could probably achieve this in three months.

This goes to show that it was a project that was well within the possibilities of a community of several hundred individuals, as the populations of the time must well have been. This type of estimate is corroborated by valuations and observations made in many different parts of the world, using comparable technical means.

The total volume of the different parts of the monument are about three times or even a little more than this initial part, that is between 6,500 and 7,000 cubic metres. Taking account of the spaces, this represents a total weight of between 12,000 and 14,000 tons. Here the time factor is even more important. For the moment however, it is difficult to say wether the building work was spread over a century, over five centuries, but the time involved could well be of that order. After all, this was often the case for the building of cathedrals.

Old postcard of the angled dolmen at Keravel in Saint-Pol-de-Léon (Finistère), which was destroyed, and its plan.

In the vegetable growing region of the Léon, the T-shaped dolmen at Kerivin to the south of Saint-Pol-de-Léon is an interesting survival, even more so that in the same commune, the fine monument of the Barrière de Keravel has not survived.

The Côtes d'Armor provide us with the last examples of passage-graves (Les Sept-Iles, on the small island of Bono, a chamber lined with false supporting stones, which no longer has its passage, must have had a corbelled structure. In any case, the monument of Tossen-ar-Run near Yvias, of which only the imposing mound is visible on a high point of the plateau, was excavated at the beginning of the century, showing that it also had a similar structure of dry-stone). At Pléneuf, on a ridge, three chambers lined with false supports in a small cairn of the same type near La Ville-Pichard, are today very damaged. At Erquy, the Ville-Hamon dolmen and cairn made of pink sandstone, which implies a certain transport of materials, are now little more than souvenirs. Many other passage-graves have completely disappeared from these coasts.

There exists an important, not to say imposing group of megalithic tombs of these types in the Channel Islands. (At La Sergenté in Jersey there are remains of tomb covered with dry-stone but at Hougue-Bie on the same island, and at Déhus on Guernesey the monuments are justifiably famous). A mention also for the monuments made of limestone in Lower-Normandy, all of which are on the Jurassic fringe of the Armorican Massif. At Vierville (Manche) the monuments are very dilapidated, but at Fontenay-le-Marmion (Calvados), near Caen, the Hoguette cairn encompasses seven tombs in a rough starlike arrangement. Even more astonishing is the monument at la Hogue, containing a dozen tombs in a similar arrangement. These are the most easterly passage-graves of the Atlantic group, and radiocarbon dating shows them as being as early as those of the Poitou region and Brittany. Putting aside small regional differences, often due to the sort of materials available, this shows the great unity of the ensemble.

INTERMEDIARY TYPES
AND GALLERY-GRAVES IN BRITTANY

A small group of megalithic constructions, in South East Brittany, appears to be related to some huge monuments in the Loire basin. These gigantic edifices were not necessarily intented for use as burial chambers, and it is difficult to assign them to either of the first categories. The famous Roche-aux-Fées at Essé (Ille-et-Vilaine) is the best example of these. This fine megalith consists of a monumental entrance with a porch, followed by a low-ceilinged passage, then a vast high chamber divided into four by transverse and lateral pillars. It makes one think of a veritable temple. In any case, its architecture is reminiscent of the construction of very big dwellings. The monument known as "la Tablette" at Cournon (Morbihan) appears to be a fragment of a construction of the same type. The principle of megalithic architecture may have equally well been applied to other ends.

We have already mentioned the V-shaped dolmen of Ty-ar-Boudiquet, near Brennilis as a beginning of a dedifferentiation, which has no separation between the passage and the chamber itself. Another similar monument is the n° 1 of the Liscuis group at Laniscat (Côtes d'Armor), also inland and at the highest point in relation to two other monuments, which are classical gallery-graves, that is to say, a long chamber with an entrance at the end, parallel walls and no variation in height below the capstones of the roof. There are remains of a few other monuments, intermediary between the two types, showing that the gallery-graves in Brittany could well have derived from the local tradition of passage-graves, at least as far as the architecture is concerned. Moreover, chronological facts are clearly in favour this derivation.

But there is one other form of derivation which goes from right-angled passage-graves to gallery-graves with side entrances. In this interesting category of monuments, the long chamber, similar to a gallery-grave, is preceded by a short passage at right angles to the main part of the monument. One fine example is at Crec'h-Quillé at Saint-Quay-Perros (Côtes d'Armor). Despite having lost its covering of capstones, it still has its mound, whose edge is faced with small vertical slabs alternating with dry-stone masonry. The side entrance is particularly distinct and facing it, one of the pillars has two protuberances forming two pairs of breasts of the goddess, protector of the dead, above a necklace. In an earth embankment nearby, at Kergüntuil in Trégastel, only the chamber remains. Three of the vertical supports are decorated with nine pairs of breasts side by side with one row of a necklace visible below some of them, and also some other motifs.

Other monuments of this category are those of Tréal at Saint-Just (Ille-et-Vilaine) which has been recently restored, and Four-Sarrazin, where the slabs bordering the mound still remain. Reminiscent of the small neighbouring megalithic chambers, it is as if there was a reciprocal influence between the two burial traditions. A mention also for the monuments of Lestriguiou at Plomeur (Finistère), and in the Côtes d'Armor, La Roche-Camio at Plédran and le Champ-Grosset at Quessoy. Some-times there are "port-hole slabs" between the side entrance and the chamber, as at Coët-Correc near Mur-de-Bretagne (Côtes d'Armor). Such slabs also existed in the monuments of Kerlescan and Kerléarec at Carnac, but the latter has completely disappeared. In one case, at Mélus near Loguivy-de-la-Mer (Côtes d'Armor), the side entrance is surmounted by a lintel-slab.

All these gallery-graves with side entrances are contemporary to classical gallery-graves

Buttressed gallery-grave of Lesconil near Poullan-sur-Mer (Finistère).

Gallery-grave with lateral entrance at Tréal near Saint-Just (Ille-et-Vilaine).

and there are many common factors between the two categories. Both types are no longer situated on high points. Gallery-graves are found throughout Brittany. Although there are as many inland as on the coast, yet they become rarer towards Eastern Brittany. They are almost always gallery-graves of a fairly classic design. The rectangular construction mound where it still exists, is edged by small vertical kerbstones, forming a border (for the V-shaped dolmen as well as the gallery-graves II and III at Liscuis near Laniscat (Côtes-d'Armor). The entrance is at one end. But where the monuments are in a good state of preservation they generally have an interior wall, which may be formed by one or several transverse supports, separating two chambers of unequal length. If these sections are completely separated, it often happens that the little chamber has no entrance at all, or just a slit; there are many examples (la Chapelle, le Lobo at Caro, le Net at Saint-Gildas-de-Rhuys (Morbihan); Kermeur-Bihan and Kerandreze at Moëlan, Luzuen at Nizon, Keriou at Gouezec (Finistère); Prajou-Menhir at Trébeurden, la Roch-Camio at Pledran (Côtes-d'Armor); la Maison-ès-Feins at Tressé (Ille-et-Vilaine). There are many gallery-graves with no apparent division (for example la Ville-Bellanger at Hénansal; la Couette and le Bourg at Ploufragan, as far as the Côtes-d'Armor is concerned). Sometimes the chamber and the antechamber are linked by an open space between two uprights, or by openings dug between the latter. In these cases they have derived from the "port-hole slabs" to be found in other regions. (Toul-an-Urs at Duault, Liscuis II and III at Laniscat, Côtes-d'Armor).

The lateral supports are sometimes doubled by lines of vertical slabs distinct from the

Gallery-grave on the beach of Kernic, near Plouescat (Finistère), seen from the rear-end. This other monumental evidence of the rising sea-level has lost all its cap-stones, but the stones demarcating the mound are still there.

borders of the construction mound, (Ile Grande, Côtes d'Armor, a monument with what appears to be a unique chamber; and monuments with a separation : le Cosquer at Goulven, le Guilliguy at Ploudalmézeau, Kerbannelec at Beuzec-Cap-Sizun, in the Finistère). The buttressed gallery-grave is a particular type where the pillars lean against each other. For Coat-Menez-Guen at Melgven, three large remaining capstones cover the whole. But at Lesconil at Poullan-sur-Mer, at Goulet-Riec at Riec, as well as at Castel-Ruffel at Saint-Goazec, Finistère, there is no sign of horizontal covering slabs, and it is doubtful whether they ever existed.

The entrance is sometimes a simple narrowing (l'Ile-à-poule at Kerbors, Côtes d'Armor, and several monuments already mentioned, Lesconil, le Mougau, Kerbannelec, l'Ile Grande), in a straight edge of mound.

Some gallery-graves have engraved or carved stones. The mother-goddess is found again on them, extremely stylized, in the form of pairs of breasts in relief, often joined (Tressé (Ille-et-Vilaine) : two scrolls, each comprising two pairs of breasts; at Commana, two pairs in two different places; at Prajou near Trébeurden, a scroll with two pairs of breasts and another slab with one pair and a necklace). At Tressé as well as Trébeurden, these decorations are in the small cell, completely separated from the chamber. Also on these stones can be discerned engravings of objects with a narrow handle, which used to be considered copper or bronze weapons but which could be any kind of object with a narrow handle, or even represent mushrooms (Prajou-Menhir, in the cell; le Mougau at Commana, on the walls of the long chamber).

At Mougau there is also a fine illustration of a stone axe with haft, and at Prajou-Menhir there are rectangles reminiscent of those on the Saint-Samson menhir. In these last two monuments, these exceptional decorations are situated on pillars which completely separate the chamber from the small cell-like part.

The gallery-grave of the Mougau (the cavern) near Commana (Finistère).

Nine pairs of breasts carved in relief, with "necklaces" carved below, in the Kergüntuil gallery-grave near Trégastel (Côtes d'Armor).

Carved axe with haft on the stone of the gallery-grave at Mougau near Commana (Finistère).

In the small chamber of the Prajou-Menhir gallery-grave at Trébeurden (near the road to the Ile Grande), a pair of breasts above a "necklace", close to another design in the form of a "palette".

THE FUNCTION AND THE GRAVE-GOODS OF MEGALITHIC TOMBS

After describing the various types of megalithic tombs, it is appropriate to demonstrate clearly their use as burial chambers, and in some cases, one might add other related and complementary functions related to variations in the quality and quantity of dead that were kept there. The "celtomanes", 150 years ago thought they saw in them druid altars or sacrificial altars with channels for the blood to run down, and also stupid ideas of this kind are in vogue nowadays in certain circles. The burial function has been illustrated every time an unexplored monument has been the subject of a scientific excavation by a serious archaeologist : when the chemical conditions allow (alkaline soil and subsoil, preferably in a limestone area, a state almost never found in Brittany, where the phosphate in the bones dissolves over thousands of years), human bones of the Neolithic period are found, often in large quantities : In passage-graves in the Poitou region and in Normandy, situated on the fringe of the Jurassic limestones, the bones of 15 to 20 individuals have been found. The gallery-graves of the Paris Basin, and the hypogeum of the same period, can contain the bones of up to 200 individuals. These bones have the same age as the monuments, and are not later additions, as confirmed by radio-carbon dating (in fact a part of the early dating of the passage-graves of the Poitou and Normandy was obtained from the bones). In Brittany, the passage-graves of Quiberon and Saint-Pierre-Quiberon, buried under sand dunes, proved to be crammed full of bones. The same applies to the small chambers of the La Torche dolmen and the chamber of the one at Roc'h-Avel. In other cases, where the covering structure acted as an umbrella and diverted rain water, fragments of bones remain, as is the case at Barnenez. At Saint-Thois, many fragments have survived. These include faggot-like bundles of long bones, scorched by flames.

The number of bones which it has been possible to discover, when they are preserved, shows that the megalithic tombs were collective, to the extent of grouping together the remains of scores or hundreds of individuals. The custom may have continued over long periods, several centuries, long after the construction of these monuments. They were the communal tombs for a whole clan, village or family, but not all the community's dead were left there. There must have been some criteria of choice. In many cases the most recently buried remains are still intact skeletons tied in a squatting position, which was probably the case when there were few burials. The older remains were piled up in a corner or stocked in some organised way. Sometimes megalithic burial chambers were only ossuaries, in the sense that once bare of flesh, the bones were heaped up. This is evident from several known cases in Northern Europe. There are nevertheless some indisputable instances of cremation (especially in Ireland), and perhaps for some of the great mounds in the Morbihan which contain closed chambers. Finally, individual tombs in small cists have sometimes been linked to the collective monuments.

At least for certain megalithic tombs of the British Isles and of Scandinavia, it has been proved that the cult of the dead involved the gruesome exhibition on certain occasions of bones of the ancestors, or sometimes from dead still in course of putrefaction, relicts that one replaced afterwards in a corner of the tomb. By their function of social integration, the open tombs permitting a permanent communication with the dead, were built as much for the living as for the defunct people.

An intact monument almost always contains personal objects in considerably varying quantities, but whose characteristics and disposition leads one to consider them as ritual "grave-goods".

The grave-goods give us most of the clues which we have about the techniques and the way of life of the megalith builders, but it is too varied in both times and space to be analyzed in detail here. As well as weapons, these grave-goods include domestic or agricultural tools, personal ornaments or jewellery, ritual objects and traces of food. So there are quarters of meat, of which nothing is left but the bones, urns filled with grain, sometimes carbonized, or drinks, probably water or beer, of which nothing remains.

All this proves that the deceased were equipped for the great journey into the next world, with a symbolic emergency supply. The fact that many of the objects, even the precious ones, have been broken, either deliberately when placed there or later during "sweepings" of the burial chambers to make room for new interments, seems to show that they were purely ritual objects. Also, when bones were taken outside for ceremonial purposes, fragments of objects in the graves may have been taken as well. Finally it must be remembered that perishable substances, including objects made of wood, bone, leather, cloth, fibres or fur, have for the most part disappeared.

We have already mentioned the particular zones of the monumental facades which were small parvis or esplanades. In these zones, the concentration of broken pottery, among other objects, is evidence of regular outside ceremonies (for example at Larcuste, at Gavrinis, at Carn or at Barnenez, to mention but some). These could of course have been ceremonies relating to "the day of the dead", but more probably there were other functions as far as the most prestigious megalithic monuments were concerned. A function of social integration for the whole community, of which the cult of the ancestors and consulting them as oracles would have only been a part. This is reinforced by the monuments being built in a dominant position over the local territory. A monument might not only have been the house of the ancestors, a temple, but in some ways might have been a community centre or some kind of "town-hall", or even "a school", if the preparation and initiation of young adolescents took place around it...

Archaeological excavations on the site of the Table-des-Marchand at Locmariaquer (summer 1987).

THE SOCIETY OF MEGALITH BUILDERS

For those prehistorians who hazard to make sociological speculations, Neolithic societies are, in principle, considered to be relatively egalitarian. The different geographically dispersed communities did not of course dispose of the same economic resources, although this did not create dependency between neighbouring communities, only normal exchanges and family links, especially where systematic exogamy (obligation to choose a partner outside ones own community) applied. Some momentary competition may have arisen, or even conflicts. It is thought that with the neolithic societies, the loss of innocence, especially in the event of demographic pressure and competition for the most fertile areas, must have degenerated into what were the first war-like conflicts, going beyond the simple local disagreements that must have always existed.

Nevertheless, the impressive size of megalithic monuments, their use for only a part of the population, and the disparity of grave-goods in some of them, all seem to indicate a beginning of social stratification. Another question is whether this budding hierarchy was the reason for the monuments having been built, or if it was the result of a phenomenon that provoked the building of these exceptional burial chambers. It is now generally thought that if megalithism was born and developed along the Atlantic coasts, it was due to factors such as the need to become more sedentary and thus more attached to a particular area, and this under the protection of the community's ancestors. The discovery of new techniques, their adaptation to the particular resources of each territory, was also accompanied by the increased know-how of a few individuals, more capable in the handling of big stones and their use in constructions. Without going as far as considering that a cast of priest-engineers developed, as some people have suggested, the general prestige of those responsible for organising such important work might well have led to a certain hierarchical system based on a certain dependency as far as the local territory was concern.

With information from archaeological documents relative to megalithic monuments and knowledge of the populations and their related technical activities, and by completing the picture with synchronous facts attested in other regions, we can try to synthesize the ideas that we have about the cultural level of the megalith builders. It was a real civilization, consisting not only of social structures organised on the hierarchical system, but also a beginning of specialization of work. The production of food in large quantities had made men more independent of the vagaries of nature, and had made possible a marked increase in population, implying the clearing of new lands in the interior of the peninsula, farther away from the coasts that were so attractive in early Neolithic times.

THE MEGALITHIC CIVILISATION IS A NEOLITHIC CIVILISATION

Despite a distribution relatively limited to the Atlantic fringes of Europe, with some momentary and reduced influence in neighbouring regions, megalithic stones and constructions are no more than a rather particular aspect or regional variation of European Neolithic civilisations, preceding them as far as their technology, economy, material culture, beliefs, social structure and ideologies are concerned. In order to have an idea of the cultural and technical level of the megalith builders, our conclusions must be based on the documents associated with these monuments, and the picture completed with proved synchronic facts in other regions where the living conditions were as comparable as possible, and take into account any differences in natural resources and weather for instance. Due to unfavourable conservation conditions in our regions, hardly anything remains of objects made of natural materials such as wood, basket-work, textiles etc. The conservation of these kinds of objects require either very dry desert-like conditions (out of the question), or a humid environment (lakes, permanent marshes, peat-bogs), such as alpine and peri-alpine lake deposits, or for example the peat-bogs of the British Isles (the Somerset Levels are the nearest). With the necessary precautions, knowledge acquired in these areas can be legitimately transposed to our regions.

The production of food in larger quantities along with improvements in its stocking and preservation had made men more independant of the vagaries of nature, and with a sedentary life-style, had made possible a marked increase in population. The population of Brittany towards the middle or late Neolithic could well have been in the order of 100, 000 inhabitants. Nevertheless, a population concentrated in villages was more at risk from the spread of infectious and viral diseases and also the inconveniences of a change of diet (eating cereals, therefore sugars, increases the incidence of dental decay).

Brittany is situated in the region of convergence of the spreading and extension of the two principal currents of Neolithic life-styles, the Mediterranean current and the so called "Danubian" current (that is coming up North of the Alps from the Balkans to the Paris Basin. French prehistorians often prefer the term "Rubané" which refers to a Western variation of Bandkeramik, the pottery of these groups, but the more general term "Danubian", is also used to designate the many secondary and later facial types).

Apart from the use of natural caves and grottos, the inhabitants of the Southern current, living on the plains, preferred relatively small dwellings on carefully worked stone foundations and whose superstructures we know little about, except the more recent ones which tended to be huts limited by small dry-stone walls. The North European current prefered large family houses with a timber framework and wattle and daub walls.

Thus in Southern Brittany, it appears that the choice was of settlements of fairly large villages, sometimes entrenched on higher ground, with houses or huts on bases of stone of which we know little about (the camp of le Lizo in Carnac; the fortified headland of Croh-Collé at Saint-Pierre-Quiberon, in the Morbihan). On the southern limit of Brittany, the camp of des Prises at Machecoul (Loire-Atlantique), situated on limestone, has late Neolithic traces of concentric and non-continuous ditches with holes for poles of the stockade, and on the inside, other holes, either for poles of houses or other stockades.

The earlier known settlements, on old land now covered by the sea along the Channel coast, were on the border of the coastal marshlands and were houses with a timber framework and wattle and daub walls. It is not known whether these houses were as big as those of the "Danubian" traditions known as far as the Paris Basin (the Aisne Valley for example). The trapezoidal plan of many of the megalithic cairns leads one to think that the houses, or at least any common dwellings, were on the same plan. These dwellings might well be reasonably comfortable, and with care and maintenance, last for 25 to 30 years.

Agricultural equipment consisted of individual tools. Polished stone axes were used to clear woodlands, and with an appropriate handle were used as hoes. Large polished stone axes were used as cutting blades or plough shares in the primitive fields. There were also stone picks (not very abundant in Brittany), picks made of deer antlers, shovels made from bovine shoulder-blades, reaping sickles made of flint blades placed side by side in a wood or bone handle and finally various other tools made of wood, which wore out quickly but were easily replaced. Farming was carried out in small garden-like fields and consisted of growing cereals (barley, wheat, millet; from burnt grains we can establish the varieties) which were eaten in the form of pancakes, bread or gruel, or drunk as barley beer. They also grew simple vegetables. The gathering of natural herbs, berries and fruit completed these resources.

They started using flax, a natural plant, to make nets and clothes. Millstones and stone pestles were used to grind grains and other vegetable foodstuffs.

Some fine polished stone axes : top left is an axe made from fibrolite; below is a heeled axe in the shape of a button made from dolerite; on the right are two axes made from jadeit, one of which has a hollowed cutting edge.

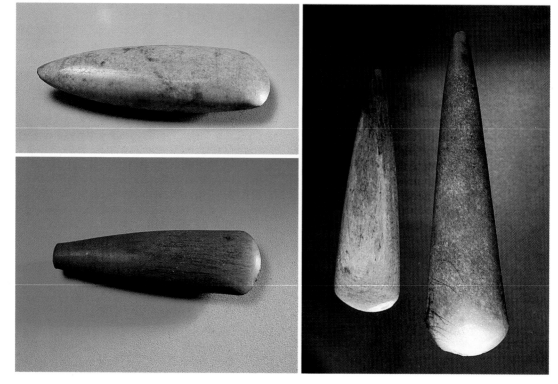

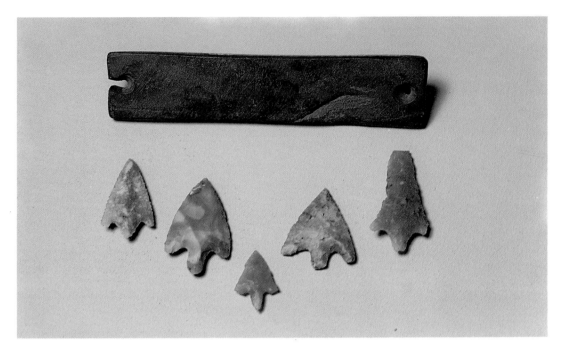

*Archer's wrist protector made of schist and flint arrow-heads and flights.
Objects of the Late Neolithic and Chalcolithic period, dating from the last
periods of reuse for funeral purposes of megalithic tombs.*

The domestication of animals concerned sheep, oxen and pigs, kept for their milk and meat, as well as their skins and horns. The figurations of the Table-des-Marchand, Gavrinis and Saint-Samson remind us of this. The dog is an old companion of man. Hunting probably continued to play an important part, and different arrow-heads indicate that small animals were hunted.

Among the domestic craft techniques, the spinning of wool, from an early form of sheep, appears in the late Neolithic with the use of spindle counter-weights made of stone or pottery. Material found in the rich lake-bed excavations show that all wood crafts were very developed as well as the use of bones and deer antlers. Dredging of the Breton rivers has brought to light axe handles made of deer antlers identical to those found in other regions. Several picks made of deer antlers have been found in sites along the Breton coasts, and flint mines are known in Calvados.

Another important domestic craft must be mentioned. The emergence of pottery is almost a definition of the Neolithic period.

As well as cooking pots, often with round bottoms and hanging handles, there were finer quality vases with varied decoration, according to the period and the tribe. So the detailed study of prehistoric pottery has become an essential basis for establishing chronologies and the relation between various civilizations. If some fragments are ubiquitous and give us little information, others tell us much. Neolithic pottery was not fired to a very high temperature, was fragile and liable to deterioration. It was hardly intended to be used on a fire. To heat water, stones heated on a fire were placed inside the wooden, leather or pottery vessel.

To make pottery of a reasonable quality is in itself a complicated technique, even when it is made by hand and then smoothed over. One needs to chose the materials. To avoid

On the top left, a vase with a hollow base from Barnenez (about 5, 000 to 6, 000 years before the present day). In the middle, a round-based vase with hanging handles from la Torche.

Bottom left is a more roughly made vase found in a gallery-grave (about 4, 000 to 4, 500 years before the present day).

Bottom right is a necked bottle from the northern dolmen on the Ile Carn, dating from the beginning of the Late Neolithic, about 4, 500 to 5, 000 years before the present.

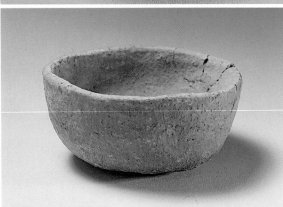

cracking during drying, an appropriate temper agent has to be added to the clay used if it does not naturally exist (in Brittany it is generally a clay resulting from the surface alteration of the rocks). Some quite strange mineralogical mixtures have sometimes been used. Alongside the rough pottery that have been discovered in the form of disparate and eroded fragments, there are fragments of finer and carefully worked pieces that deserve our admiration. Let us recall that comparative ethnography shows us that throughout the world, domestic pottery is almost always made by and used "with motherly care" by women.

The working of stone, mainly flint, is more of a masculine occupation. All kinds of cutting tools were made, used rough-cut as knives, or reworked to be used as scrapers, arrow-heads and other various tools. Right at the end of the Neolithic period, the working of stone reached its peak with the use of light-coloured flint imported from Touraine, used as it was or made into slavish imitations of copper daggers which were beginning to circulate. Previous to this, they imported finished or rough polished axes, using flint from Normandy or the Charente region. An old massif like Brittany has no natural sources of flint except a few poor small pebbles from the off-shore bars of the beaches. Nevertheless, whether in megalithic monuments or in dwellings, this beach flint has been found in quite large quantities in the form of small unworked fragments of little interest and some larger pieces showing that its cutting qualities must have had some importance.

The working of hard eruptive or metamorphic rocks, by chipping, roughening and polishing, opened up many new possibilities far beyond those of the few outcrops of quartzite used on a small scale to replace flint. Probably during hunting expeditions, and with a certain geological flair, the men of Neolithic Brittany found a few outcrops of rocks that were better than others. The result was a whole range of axes and adzes and other objects. These were finely worked and polished on either large fixed stones or even with small hand-held tools.

One hesitates to assign to the influence of the Neolithic Central European "Danubian" cultural current, the drilled types of instruments such as hammer-axes made of hard rocks. In any case, these instruments became frequent in the Late Neolithic, at the same time as finely finished "battle-axes" that imitated the copper prototypes of Eastern Europe, a fashion spread by the civilisations of Central and Northern Europe. In Brittany, variations of these prestigious objects were often naviform (boat-shaped) bipennate (double cutting edge) axes. Most of our knowledge of these comes from fragments and fabrication "rejects" (drilling the cylindrical hole was a delicate operation).

The quarrying of suitable rocks became a real industry, for the most prized materials. More than one third of the Breton polished axes can only come from the same outflow of dolerite, located in Côtes-d'Armor, at Plussulien. A quarry was established around a rock, and the adjoining workshops produced rough-cut articles for almost 1, 500 years without interruption. Once finished, these products were exported mainly to the Paris Basin but also as far as Southern England, Belgium, Alsace, the Rhone Valley and Aquitaine. A dyke of hornblendite, located near Pleuven (Finistère) was to make battle-axes found throughout the Armorican peninsula, the Seine and Loire Basins, and as far away as the Netherlands. Several Breton seams of fibrolite, a rock that can only be cut or polished, were exploited, especially at the entrance to the Morbihan Gulf and at Plouguin in the North Finistère (of which some products crossed the Channel). So from various "factories", a long distance trade distributed tonnes of raw materials and artefacts, in exchange for which other things were imported. Tools or weapons for display (axes of jadeit and eclogite), jewellery or ornaments (beads and pendants of variscite (callaïs = a precious stone, variscite is known from the Loire-Atlantique department), at Pannecé; veritable Neolithic mines are known in Catalonia; flat rings of jadeit and serpentine) in rare and precious materials, are of less certain origin.

One used to believe in vague regional possibilities for certain materials such as eclogites, but recent sophisticated analyses show these rocks are of alpine origin like the jadeitites (the beautiful green jadeitites), probably from the Piemont or similar regions. Quantities of these came down the Rhine Valley and are found in Germany and neighbouring countries, and as far as England and Scotland. Without importing these objects from Asia, as was believed a century ago, it is clear that the common market of prestigious objects in Western Europe had been operating for some time. Nevertheless, bartering between neighbouring tribes did involve fairly long distances and times.

Right at the end of the Neolithic period in our regions (not forgetting that our Neolithic was contemporary with the Copper Age in Eastern Europe), the existence of rare tools and weapons made of arsenated copper and even bronze, in particular little tanged daggers, shows that certain megaliths were used or erected at the time of the first widespread use of metal (Chalcolithic period) closely linked to the campaniform (bell-beaker) vases. Local gold was also used for ornaments, generally in the form of wire or leaves produced by beating nuggets found in rivers (Brittany was quite rich in gold bearing alluvium).

Necklace of variscite pearls.

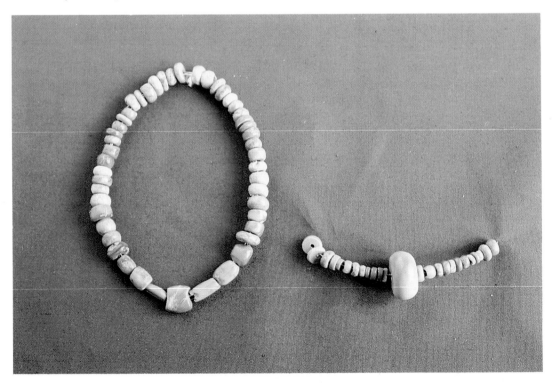

CHRONOLOGICAL POSITION OF THE MEGALITHIC MONUMENTS

Now that the broad outlines of the civilization of the megalith builders have been revealed, it remains to date it more exactly in time and to place it against the scale of the prehistoric periods. Compared to the long history of mankind this is comparatively recent, at the end of the prehistoric period of our region, at the turning point of protohistory. For several thousand years, somewhere in the near East, the great Neolithic economic revolution had already substituted for a precarious life based on hunting, fishing or gathering food, a more stable existence based on the intentional production of food. A remark in passing. At more or less the same time and independently, in other regions of the world, similar innovations were in progress (rice growing in the Far East, maize in Central America, etc). From this had resulted a series of technical advances, and when this economic revolution spread to western Europe, it was no longer in its initial stages, and in fact the Europeans themselves had imagined complementary changes to these new life-styles. But at that moment a new development had occured in the Eastern regions, and was entering history with writing. Part of this new progress, spreading even more quickly, was beginning to make itself felt in the West.

Western megalithic culture was one of these European innovations. Thanks to the prodigious contribution of scientific information amassed over the last forty years we are now able to measure time more accurately. By far the most precise method of dating is dendrochronology, the counting of growth rings of trees. This allows accuracy to a year up to 7, 000 years back, subject of course to having conserved wood deposits, preferably oak (in central European lakes and Ireland for example). It allows other dating methods to be corrected. Of these, radiocarbon dating is the most used (radiocarbon dating does not measure time in the same way as absolute time, therefore it needs to be corrected by dendrochronology). Radiocarbon dating gives us "ranges" or "slices" of time in which we place archaeological or geological events. The same applies to other physico-chemical dating methods. Among others, these include thermoluminescence methods applied to pottery.

Thanks to the prodigious contribution of information obtained by the radiocarbon method of dating, and thanks to the comparative study of all the data of the problem, it can now be said that the megalithic graves of Armorica, which may have had prototypes elsewhere several centuries older, first appeared about 7, 000 years ago, and perhaps even earlier. They were built over a period of between 2, 500 and 3, 000 years and probably remained in use until more or less 3, 800 to 4, 000 years ago, differing from one place to

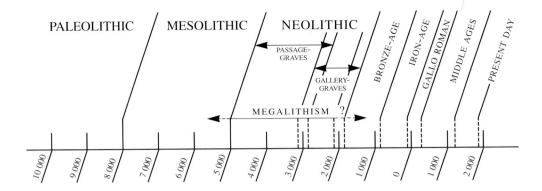

another according to circumstances, local traditions and the temptations to reuse them.

These evaluations are almost double those that were currently given thirty years ago, which have been progressively revised. Without going into too much detail, for a long time there were technical reasons for using only dates B.P. (Before Present, blocked arbitrarily at 1950 A.D.) and avoiding references to B.C. which implied comparisons with historical dates. Recent progress in methods of correction (calibration), between 1981 and 1985, now allows to compare events using the normal method of counting time (but this explains why meanwhile in some more or less recent works there can be apparent contradictions or discrepancies. To illustrate it must be remembered that 1000 years of radiocarbon may correspond to only 950 sidereal years or 1, 500 sidereal years, according to the time zones being studied).

It is therefore now possible to specify the sequence of the different types of megalithic tombs in Brittany, and also the different types of pottery that allow us to establish the characteristic of the successive phases of the Neolithic period in Brittany. Knowing that pre-megalithic pottery appeared in the Vendée region and in West-Central France towards 5, 500 years B.C., this fixes the beginnings of neolithisation at about the same time as in the Rhinelands and in the Benelux region, whereas at the same time the hunter-fishermen of Brittany were still piling up their remains of food on heaps of sea-shells and perhaps were beginning to domesticate some animals.

Therefore, the first passage-graves began to be built at least towards 5, 000 years B.C., and a little later were associated with the first old western form of Neolithic type pottery of our regions, called Carn type pottery. This pottery, sometimes very fine with a carefully smoothed surface rather like a piece of leather, consists of round-bottomed vases which were sometimes decorated with applied rolls of clay. In the same phase, in Eastern and Southern Brittany, there are traces of grooved or stippled decoration indicating a link with pottery types of the "Danubian" civilisations which had then reached as far as the Paris Basin, Normandy and the Channel Islands. In Poitou and in the Vendée, on the other hand, we find a variant of the Carn type, called the Cous type. This type also consist of globulous round-bottomed and carefully made vases, but which often have a narrowing at the neck. All these types of pottery have in common a rounded base. They were not intended to be stood up.

Passage-graves continue, with multiple variations, more often than not regional, and develop towards either those with lateral chambers or partitions, or those with less differentiation between the chamber and the passage. In these we find more diversified and more decorated pottery, though still with a rounded base. On the one hand there is an evolution of the Carn type, leading to the Souc'h type, with vertical perforated handles, and the Quélarn, type with button-like decorations around the opening. On the other hand an even stronger influence of the so-called Chassey cultures of South and Central France of the Middle Neolithic period, leading to a Breton form of pottery with a shoulder between the body and the neck, and also a special kind of highly decorated vase, sort of cup on stand (formerly called vases support). It is also at this time that articles that existed previously, such as polished axes appear, but were not yet put with the grave-goods (in abundance in the closed chambers of the great tumuli of the region of Carnac and Locmariaquer).

The last of the classical series of passage-graves were built a little after 4, 000 years B.C. at the same time as a certain number of derived variations, such as right-angled monuments. Then, towards 3, 500 years B.C., differentiated monuments appeared, followed by tombs whith lateral entrances and finally gallery-graves. The last of the gallery-graves may have been built around 2, 500 years B.C. With these different types are associated different kinds of regional pottery, with the development of flat-bottomed pots. On the South coast, from the Finistère to the South of the Loire-Atlantique, one finds pottery of the Kerugou type, with a vertical or re-entrant neck with moulded or incised vertical decorations. Further North, one generally finds Quessoy type pottery, with no vertical decorations. And finally, pottery of the Neolithic styles of the Paris Basin called, S.O.M., introduced into Brittany large rough vases such as "flower-pots" and variations of "collared-bottles". After the relatively unified style of the Middle Neolithic, the period of the tombs of the passage-grave type, came the Recent and Late Neolithic with a diversification of types with either the continued use of pre-existing monuments (sometimes modified or added to) or a certain tribalisation.

One last important phase of reuse of megalithic tombs, probably involving little or no construction, was in the Chalcolithic, a long phase of transition between economies using stone tools and those using metal ones. Associated with this period are the so-called campaniform beakers (upside down bell-beakersor) and other related articles characteristic of this cultural entity. There was a tendency to relate these bell-beakersor beakers to a new population, but now they are seen more as an expression of a political fashion or taste for prestigious objects, and might have been used to drink special liqueurs. They begin at about 2, 500 years B.C. in our regions.

Megalithism must therefore be perceived in a long term perspective. Even without taking into account the earliest attempts of construction, of which little is known, from the technical indications and identifiable remains of constructions in Breton Bronze Age tumuli we can say that megalithism covers at least a period of 2, 500 years. This is much longer than historical times of Gaule and France, showing that it was not a short-lived fashion.

But megaliths are almost recent seen in the perspective of the three million years of the natural and primitive history of mankind. Everything distinguishes them from the civilizations which lasted thousands of years, during the Palaeolithic period, during which mankind slowly took its first steps. No confusion can remain in people's minds, and the word prehistoric should not necessarily evoke Neanderthal man or cave paintings. Conversely, immediately after the megaliths, right in the Bronze Age, the Armoricain peninsula knew a protohistoric civilization very different in essence, before passing into the Iron Age, and then into History.

Monuments as extraordinary as the mega-liths retained well beyond their hey-day a cultural significance or a mythical aura for the early tribes, and an attraction or a repulsion for later arrivals in the region. So the

Armoricans of the Iron Age infiltrated occasional graves in some burial chambers, and the Gallo-Romans searched and plundered a large number of them. They installed graves or sanctuaries in them or celebrated chtonian rituals there, as if they were natural caves. At all times since the Bronze Age, standing stones have always been used as landmarks for hiding places for treasure or for organising the countryside. Beliefs and rituals during protohistoric and antique times were marked by a tendency towards syncretism, that is a fusion of ideas and traditions.

Finally and above all, Christian priests and missionaries, continually coming up against the irresistible attraction of the Bretons to these stones, tainted with an ancestral paganism and still fiercely potent, had them destroyed, mutilated or buried, but most often attempted to "Christianize" them. This policy of cultural assimilation and appropriation is marked sometimes by the addition or the engraving of crosses and other symbols, sometimes by the incorporation into a religious building (burial chamber in the crypt of La Chapelle des Sept-Saints, at Vieux-Marché (Côtes-d'Armor), sometimes by the moving and inclusion of the monument in a consecrated enclosure.

The example of the life of Saint Samson is edifying. Having left Wales to come to Brittany, he crossed Cornwall, where he found the local people dancing around a standing stone. He severely rebuked them and had the stone destroyed or mutilated. But when he arrived on the other side of the Channel, he established his monastery at Dol, in the proximity of the great standing stone of the Champ Dolent, which he left untouched (but may have crowned it with a cross). He also left alone the great stone situated on the other side of the Rance, in a parish bearing his name and belonging to his monastery

Christianized menhir on the Lande de Cojoux, Saint-Just.

Menhir of Saint-Duzec at Pleumeur-Bodou.

Louisfert (Loire-Atlantique).

(although perhaps he was responsible for digging a hole at its foot, which explains the stone' s angle. It is said that a cone and an iron ring were once found there).

But a folklore cannot be converted, and this christianization, although sometimes effective, was often superficial. In fact only recently, a number of megaliths occupied a high position among the legend-stones of Brittany, to which various strange pagan practices were attached, sometimes coated with a veneer of Christianity. However it would be wrong to think that the origins of this folklore of the stones can be traced back to the era of the builders of the megalithic monuments. There have been many successive civilizations between us and them.

However, the tombs and the standing stones which are so numerous in Brittany remain nevertheless the venerable remains of a lost civilization, of an already advanced level. All in all, our civilisation is hardly more advanced. It would be a complete mistake to assume that at the time the people were "barbarians". They may well have lived peacefully, in relative safety and generally fraternal most of the time.

These stones, grouped into burial monuments or standing like mysterious symbols, are one of the most moving and perhaps the most important testimonies in Europe, or even perhaps in the whole world, left by tribes who had a complete system of beliefs and rites. Towards these people we owe great debt, although we do not always recognise it.

So these huge stones standing upright on the horizon, out on the moors, still demand today, if not the respect and astonishment which they deserve, at least the legitimate curiosity of the passer-by.

Rennes and Penmarc'h, 1957-1992.

BIBLIOGRAPHIE

P.-R. GIOT, J. MONNIER, J. L'HELGOUACH : Préhistoire de la Bretagne, O.F. , 1979.

P.-R. GIOT, J. BRIARD, L. PAPE : Protohistoire de la Bretagne, OF, 1979.

P.-R. GIOT, BATT, LECERF, LECORNEC et LE ROUX : Au pays des Mégalithes, Editions Jos, 1985.

P.-R. GIOT : Barnenez, un grand cairn mégalithique, Editions Jos, 1987.

J. BRIARD : Mégalithes de Bretagne, O.F, 1987.

P.-R. GIOT : Les alignements de Carnac, O.F. , 1983.

C.-T. LE ROUX : Gavrinis et les îles du Morbihan, Imprimerie Nationale, 1985.

Gw. LE SCOUEZEC : Bretagne mégalithique, Seuil, 1987.

A. BURL : Mégalithic Brittany a Guide, Thames and Hudson, 1985.

D. ROCHE : Carnac, Tchou, 1973, Suger, 1985.

J.L. MONNIER : Préhistoire de la Bretagne et d'Armorique, Gisserot 1991.

Achevé d'imprimer sur les presses des Imprimeries CLOITRE à Saint-Thonan en mars 1993.
Dépôt légal : mars 1993.
ISBN : 2-85543-123-9